Ring the Bells

Also by Colleen Keating and published by Ginninderra Press

A Call To Listen
(Shortlisted, Society of Women Writers NSW Book Awards 2016)

Fire on Water
(Highly Commended, Society of Women Writers NSW Book Awards 2018; Nautilus Award – Silver 2017)

Hildegard of Bingen: A poetic journey
(Winner, Poetry, and Winner, Non-fiction, Society of Women Writers NSW Book Awards 2020; Nautilus Award, Silver, 2019)

Desert Patterns
(Highly Commended, Poetry, Society of Women Writers NSW Book Awards 2020)

Olive Muriel Pink: Her radical and idealistic life: A poetic journey
(Highly Commended, Poetry, Society of Women Writers NSW Book Awards 2022)

Beachcomber

The Dinner Party

Soft Gaze, with Michael Keating (Picaro Poets)

Brush of Birds (Picaro Poets)

Landscapes of the Heart, with John Egan (Picaro Poets)

Shared Footprints, with Michael Keating (Picaro Poets)

Mood Indigo, with Pip Griffin (Picaro Poets)

Mists of Time, with Decima Wraxall (Pocket Poets)

Ring
the Bells

Colleen Keating

*To our grandchildren, Lachlan, Thomas, Tyler, Jacinta,
Cameron, Edison, Dominic, Eleanor, Gemma,
Darcy and Ethan.*

May they always hear the bells ring.

Ring the Bells
ISBN 978 1 76109 715 7
Copyright © text Colleen Keating 2025
Cover image by Graham Davidson

First published 2025 by
GINNINDERRA PRESS
PO Box 2 Bentleigh 3204
ginninderrapress.com.au

Contents

Ring the Bells

Introduction   9

Embracing light

Mahler's song	13
resurrection	14
gratitude	15
pondering	16
a mystery to fathom	18
after William Carlos Williams	19
Fifth symphony	20
mango	21
Le Ciel	22
Hyde Park dusk	23
between breaths	24
my oracle	26
bells	28
informed by a landscape	29

Embracing dark

Daybreak at Mt. Sondar (Rwetyepme)	33
Curio	34
day of mourning	36
cry my people	37
windows for miracles	38
intrusion	39
Shadows	40
dream-burden	42

Ukraine	43
against the odds	45
in memory of Uvalde's children	46
canary warning	48
ode to soil	49
loud fence	51
Hebrew Chorus	52
I can't breathe	54
afterwards	55

Embracing life

portal	58
winter days	59
decluttering	60
messages	61
wood pigeon	62
sanctum	63
epiphany	64
nankeen kestrel	66
waiting for godwits	67
delusions of grandeur	69
mirror on mirror	70
Murphy's law	71
eve time	72
bronze bells	74
Two Canticles	75

Embracing love

a pelican-distance apart in covid times	79
the visit	83
whisper	85
tanka	86

a meeting	87
while doing a grocery shop	89
shared umbrella	90
diagnosis	91
presence	92
petal by petal	94
his favourite shirt	98
maybe a cypher	99
reminder	100
songlines	102
From the Dust of Stars	103
Celtic Knots	104
Acknowledgments	106

Introduction

> Ring the bells that still can sing
> Forget your perfect offering
> There is a crack, a crack in everything
> That's how the light gets in
> Leonard Cohen, 'Anthem'

One of my favourite paintings is The Angelus (L'Angélus) by Jean-François Millet (1857) where the peasants stand in a golden bountiful field, hats off, heads bowed. My mind's ear hears the bells. In those days, many dropped what they were doing at midday to pray.

I like the idea of ringing bells to signify times of joy; like the ringing out of an old church bell in Beaconsfield, Tasmania, after the safe rescue of the miners after nearly two weeks (bells not rung since the end of World War II); the toll in sorrow at a solemn funeral procession; in times of hope as when a replica of the excavated ancient Bronze Bells in Wuhan's Hubei Museum chimed at the turn of the century, like the the gong of a temple bell.

An enduring memory is when I rang the Peace Bell in Hiroshima Peace Park in Japan in 2012, which stands beneath the enigmatic statue of the young Sadako holding high the golden crane as a symbol of peace.

Bells were a beautiful part of my childhood. I loved to be the one to ring the bells for the Angelus at school. I can't remember if I was chosen or if I enthusiastically volunteered. It meant leaving class and being ready at midday to begin with three sets of three bells with a count of a slow twenty seconds between and then nine wonderful tolls. There was an awesome sense of satisfaction.

I can meditate for hours on the quiet arrival and temporary state of being and the idea of transformation in Buson's haiku:

> stopping to sleep
> on the temple bell –
> a butterfly

I like to think of each poem in this collection sounding a bell chime as my words embrace light, dark, life and love – cyclic like the seasons.

In our day-to-day moments we live in a broken world with personal and collective emotions, pain of war and human travail that can bring us to our knees, but beauty of nature and grace of humanity is our balm.

The Bianzhong of Marquis Yi of Zeng known as the Zenghouyi Bells made in 433 BC and unearthed in 1978.

Embracing light

drifting cloud —
her small hand traces
angels wings

Mahler's song

for Michael

if you love for beauty
do not love me
love the sun with its comfort and warmth

if you love for youth
do not love me
love the springtime that comes new to you each year

if you love for wealth
do not love me
love the ocean with its treasures and pearls

if you love for love ah yes love me
love me forever
and I will love you for evermore

Adapted from the 4th movement of the 5th Symphony

resurrection

from dark mysterious swamp
thick with paperbarks lantana and lilies

like a freight train cutting
through air in a country town

closer   like individual carriages
clanking past

closer still   rumbling –
breaking into distinctive croaks

yes the swamp is thickly alive
with a merriment of frogs

a bass chorus carousing courting
chatting   all excited to have ascended

with the rain
from an underbelly secret world

gratitude

i.m. John Egan

sometimes it takes stillness
of death to remind us to breathe
consciously

sometimes it takes silence
of air to remind us to sing
joyfully

sometimes it takes loss
of a dear one to remind us
what we have

today fluting music of birds –
tiny wrens amidst the scrub
honeyeaters after nectar

makes me pause take stock
remember a poet whose words
over and over remind us

to value the light
and now on this autumn day
in the afternoon sun

the bush is lit
with golden banksia cones
bush candles for the way

pondering

each morning i reach up
to the allure of coffee cups
hanging by hooks
shiny   empty   waiting

each morning my hand picks
the one with the chip in the rim
like one is drawn to the comfort
of a familiar friend
like one's eye is caught
by the flawed piece
in the stained-glass window

coffee filled – i'm warmed
by the art nouveau sketch
of the Eiffel Tower
with its faded scrawl
J'aime Paris

its porcelain handle soothes
the roasted aroma teases
before my first sip

teal ducks
float on pink azaleas
reflections

a mystery to fathom

who writes the scribbly dialect
etched into trunks of eucalypts?

i watch patiently –
no sign of a scribe

who is the hidden creator?
i run my finger along the rambling lines

a story to decipher
like the tag *Eternity*

left on city streets
a mystery to fathom

this scrawl gave May Gibbs
inspiration for her writing

Judith Wright peeled back
the splitting bark and mused

of this life i could not read

who is this secret poet
this graffiti artist

leaving their tag on trees
writing their journey for us?

Science has long now solved the mystery: a brown moth rarely seen is the curio. Its tiny eggs hatch, mysterious larvae burrow down like children in class taking up their pen. They tunnel along writing their journey and the circle of life comes around to form moths and like students they graduate and fly free.

after William Carlos Williams

so much depends
upon

yellow buttermilk
a weed

the blue monarch
alights

in the sun-
drenched field

Fifth symphony

Vaughan Williams
composed his symphony
on fire watch

barrages of bombs dropped
nightly   enflamed his city
no air raid shelter

for him as he pocketed
his note pad and pen
fought the crucible

of siren-moans
cries for help
and from the dark

composed music that plays
like a mountain brook
tumbling

in a moment
that brims
with tomorrow

mango

is a warm yellow heart
with fragrance
of a summer's day

its smooth curved skin
holding in
juicy flesh

bursts
with sunshine

Le Ciel

It's not 'brothers, we must die,' it is rather, 'brothers, we must live'

about light and colour he was never wrong
Henri Matisse knew from his youth
their startling wonder
how they exude an authority like a good armchair
how they uplift human nature
when the world weighs low
and how when clouds of war
dim the sun
their illumination of hope can be forgotten
as in deepest night
it is easy to forget dawn returns

in Matisse's Le Ciel
the lightness of joy fills the blue air
with a patchwork of his blues –
light and dark
alternating in and out
his cut-out sculptures of birds
float on the air
lift up   dive   whirl   spin
ethereal in white
and dancing stars glint like enamel
or they could be flowers of joy
bordered by acanthus leaves
swaying hypnotically
reminding us to live

Hyde Park dusk

it was when we saw salmon clouds
riffling the pool of reflection

that we looked up to catch them –
sylvan maids to a low super moon

tessellated by the fine tracery
of winter trees

cathedral spires
glowed a soft orange

immersed in a Turner landscape
to reach out one's hand would be to touch

a hundred hues of light   untouchable
for we were part of the light

lifting away pale and fading
into the blue air brush of a Norham Castle

not even two seagulls landing
on the pool with their swirls

could disturb the stillness
but returned our eyes

to the ineffable interaction
of light and water

and in the park
lively and real we walked on

drawing out the quiet that held us
into the chill of the evening

between breaths

an out-breath sigh settles
us to stillness
a subtle space between
the pulse of two bells

into a dappled world
ferns   palms   mossy outcrops
lanterns of red fuchsias
sienna-orange beacons of banksia

we pass sturdy trees
sentinels tall and straight
others like lazed-back friends
in their sculptured shapes –

red gums   iron bark   turpentines
their thickened roots flow
like treacle into rock crevices
amidst gold-glint

and spangle of greens
ring of whipbirds
rustles of undergrowth
alert us to wallabies

a creek of red dragonflies
sings a timpani of stones to
rhythmic raking of brush turkeys
warble of magpies   while a kookaburra

is a zen buddhist on a nearby bough
too soon   the whir of traffic
grind of machines brings
a reluctant in-breath sigh

my oracle

i visit a special tree
a regular confidante
and ponder
what this new year may bring

rooted in place
sturdy   strong
calm today
it gazes upwards
and out over the valley
as if it could see
far beyond our horizon
one thing was different

last visit its trunk was pink
sleek   inviting my hand to run
across its smooth dimply skin
today its trunk   rough
its bark splitting shedding
peeling in strips and curls
burnished as a rusty drum
exposing chartreuse rawness

i square my shoulders   stand taller
nod understanding
and thank tree wisdom
for its perfect message

For many, the Angophora Costata is commonly known as the Sydney red gum. The angophora is a special tree to the Dharug people who are the Traditional Custodians of the area. The angophora was an ascension tree, a place where the spirits would go up and down from this earthly plane.

bells

they are the sound of stones tinkling in a brook high in the hills
a lamb's urgent cry for its lost mother   jingle
of coins in a child's pocket at the door to a lolly shop

and if you can imagine the hum of a bee
with your ear to the tree touch its hairpin sound
if you can hear the toll of marching feet fade

and hear a mother lay war medals on a cedar dresser
and the rain on corrugated tin in the depth of a gun-metal sky
then you know too the clang of a door slammed in your face

and the silence that reverberates   you could know
the peal of children laughing in a school yard
or the clatter of a grandchild's cereal-laden plate on the tiles

as he in his high chair claps with delight
you might even know the rain drops spilling from leaf to leaf
in the old elm tree   and the butcher-birds' warble in the eucalypt

igniting the dawn   perhaps you hear grains of sand sifting
through the narrow neck in the soft light of a dying day
and the knell of rocks in a river on its slow flow to the sea

informed by a landscape

from the jetty the sun's fingers curl away
in colourful coat it slinks behind the Wattigan hills
bowing out like an actor at the end of a show
leaving its props strewn about the stage

here where its aftermath
pulverises sky and lake
swallows flirt with buzz of insects
above the drying wrack

its shenanigans leave a stricken sky
its last breaths like a deep bruised sigh
the heavy hills in silhouette
like cut-out cardboard children's craft

pelicans wing languidly past
tipped in salmon glow
reminding me a world is turning
whatever time is left

a lone egret creates small ripples near the edge
its reflection sharpened as the lake stills
there is a lingering here
it is all about the light

Embracing dark

stillness
an old platypus creek
dammed

Daybreak at Mt. Sondar (Rwetyepme)

in the beginning
air static as a nylon petticoat
pulled over my hair
fingerprints of ruby red
betray the world   dark coloured
the arc of dawn flexes
stirs Rwetyepme,
an awakening blush
flutters fire red   catching
Namatjira's mountain
blood red

as i sit here   it pulsates
the sun not yet over the horizon
like an intruder rushes in
steals every shade and shadow

this mountain lies in the country with poise
immortalised in a gown of purple and blue
a sleeping goddess behind glass

yet the rattle of chains and padlock
thump a heart beat against my ribs
as in the nearby town
for a dollar
kids still buy a rusty jam tin of petrol

Curio

Queen Gooseberry's mug c. 1800

Along a dim corridor of Mitchell Library, in a small alcove
a simple curio sits – a mug, small as a clenched fist
unpretentious, made of copper, brazed billycan handle.
Its story waiting to be heard.

I would hold it in my hand but like sleeping beauty,
glass has it captive. It sits on a raised block, its dull-
green metallic sheen, slipstreams my mind back two
hundred years. One can only imagine its tinkle

carried by Kaaroo, daughter of Moorooboora, sweet
wild, cultivated girl, dubbed Queen Gooseberry
caught in two worlds – to create Aboriginal 'leaders'
and 'civilise the tribes.'

When her dark hands raised the mug to receive
her allowance of rum, did she feel privilege at
the Governor's pleasure or bitter sup gripping
her belly? When smallpox raged, when curling

smoke along the coves diminished, when 'royalty'
became a failed experiment, and when her man
King Bungaree died, who in his last years worked
to quell drunken brawls in the fetid streets of early

Sydney, did anyone notice her song go silent?
Roaming the streets of Sydney Cove, she circled
each day to her own rhythm, too far removed from
her people to return.

Often sketched, mantled in her government-
issued blanket, clay pipe between tight lips, her rum
mug, a poison chalice dangled from her belt.
Did anyone notice the 'Queen' become the curio?

A scruple of remorse found the 'Queen' dead
at the back of Soldiers Inn, in the winter of 1852.
Now from this mantel through a brume of silence
the tinkle of copper portents a jangle of chains.

day of mourning

the mess of now
long-time silence textured into stone
falls lagan-like into a sea of my mind
i didn't know the truth

at the age of nine
taken to Farm Cove
with a sense of childlike pride
a mind open fresh as a shucked oyster
we sang God Save the Queen
as the Union Jack was raised

i wrote the story for Social Studies
excited at our country's prosperity
and my comfortable place in it
i didn't know the truth

years later
with a sense of shame i heard
the men who did the re-enactment
feet stamping the blooded sand
were bused in   as locals had refused

Only now I wonder
were their eyes empty
dulled by dispossession
I am learning the truth

cry my people

we watch the marches around the world
BLM banners held high
we watch with detachment of distance
wanting these cries to stay
far away
knowing enquiry after enquiry
of our own deaths in custody
are right here
quietened by apathy
silenced by the next news feed
knowing that silence cannot reign
justice has a long bow bending
to boomerang back

On hearing 602 Indigenous people have died in custody since the Royal Commission into Deaths in Custody was handed down in 1991

windows for miracles

(When a baby was rescued from the rubble, 150 hours after the Türkiye and Syria earthquake)

windows for miracles
open hands dig
exposed in corruption and winter freeze
brute force against crushed
walls of concrete

windows for miracles
rimy pictures extort tears
tiny pockets of air save
and in renascence we all
breathe humanity's ache

windows for miracles
closed hard as steel shutters
trapped against meaning
some scramble under rubble of news
grass and birds stone-walled

windows for miracles
a cry muffled by dust
tears of exhausted men
mingle in white ash of cement
halt a despairing world

intrusion

and a WARNING

                        the following contains scenes
                        that may disturb some viewers
                        discretion is advised

Ah says the screen *gotcha*

                        disarmed
                        i rummage for the remote
                        behind cushions under piles of paper
                        and flick to another channel

flip back   in time to hear
the newsreader gloat
if this has distressed…

                        tipped you over the tipping point
                        overwhelmed your overwhelming life
                        sunk you even deeper into the pit

you can contact LIFELINE
or 1800RESPECT

back to the news

                        no longer raising the shock flag

another woman is murdered today
indigenous incarceration ratio increased
2,000 feared drowned in Pakistan flood
and a new cat show
where cats learn to walk tight ropes

Shadows

(Women and children flee their homelands once again)

1.

After the deluge the track is heavy, hard-going
shoes muddied, bogs to be side-stepped.

Yet there is grace in the morning walk
with light breaking through unzipped clouds.

The bush smiles, as a slow waltz
shimmers through leaves.

Vibrant red gums stand friendly sentinels.
Brackened rocks cry with dew.

I lean against a familiar trunk of a coachwood
reassured by its sturdy cool presence.

A shadow crosses my path.
I look up –
a yellow-crested cockatoo.

2.

Meanwhile she is trudging today,
fleeing for her life
and life of her child

on frozen earth, along cold corridors,
no time to glance back. Homes

surrendered to desecration. The air cries
for her wounded homeland.

Let us imagine people welcoming her
with soup, hot bread and someone

to ease her burden. Let warm eyes greet her
and reassure her with prepared shelter.

When a shadow crosses her path
and she huddles, cowers, whimpers
let her and her child be safe

for she is everywoman.

dream-burden

it's four in the morning
and I'm awake

my great-great grandchildren
won't let me sleep

they ask over and over
what did you do when the earth was suffering

when the rivers were dying
how did you act

when the insect world was disappearing
when the icebergs began to melt

and what woke me was the free-
fall cry of answering

Ukraine

'I think it better that at times
like these we poets
keep our mouths shut.'
– W.B. Yeats (from 'On being asked for a war poem' 1919)

i cannot be silent
in this sorrow of war
the enemy has raised its monstrous head
where decency gives way
to rage that leads to war that leads to rage
...and this too will end

leaders will make deals   shake hands
some will put aside propaganda
and become allies
once again trenches filled in
old war tanks disassembled
in time they will build a cenotaph
engrave the names of heroes –
not the women   old men   children
displaced and broken
not victims who paid the price
as the English FTSE and Russian MOEX
surge with shareholder profits
and each touts
winner!

no one gains land
for there is nothing to gain
it's all an illusion   despots deceived
yet there is a lot to lose   leaving
values diminished   sadness in a mother's eyes
fear in a child's heart
hate and revenge replacing a teenager's dreams
the loss of decency in the soldier

meanwhile the sun anchors
this tiny dot in the ocean of sky
and its lens blinks
another 'lest we forget'

against the odds

at first it is only human hands
humanities howl across agony

search and find with stinging tears of joy
then terror cowers to machinery

search and rescue stills like the silence
of a stillborn

search and recover cosseted
in black plastic bags

then the rescue – a plaster-white stiff
statued-man fights the black darkness

of the shroud with gasps of sweet air
drinking urine while it flowed

he said drinking his own urine
kept hope alive

in memory of Uvalde's children

our once big world   now a global village
with space and time a lilliput in a satellite realm
is real   its song of humanity
its agonising cry

today's message carries
visions of a school shooting
only past school photos left –
tiny faces peering out
their shining eyes
show all the little dreams
children dream
and strip to nakedness
a whole nation
staring once again at emptiness

we are the witness
with adults bent over in pain
– many in foetal position
holding their bodies
from its bloodbath

it is said giving attention
is the rarest and purest sense of generosity
focus on a small town a primary school
focus on a classroom   children
focus on the good   alive in the agony of dissent
weaving   weaving   weaving in

On 24 May 2022, an 18-year-old gunman wielding an AR-15-style rifle killed 19 children and two teachers at Robb Elementary School in Uvalde, Texas, a small city west of San Antonio. It was the deadliest school shooting since 20 children and six adults were killed at Sandy Hook Elementary School in Connecticut in 2012.

canary warning

the plane to Cairns hugs the coast
spectacular views beguile
while a drama unfolds below

the skin of the earth
is ripped raw
its wounds bleeding

a bitter-red brown surge
breaks into expanse of sea
at each river outlet

life-threatening haemorrhage
a little known warning for our planet
only birds know

it does not have a song
unless you hear red cry of wind
unless you see troubled rivers

unless you face the stifled
silence of slaughtered trees
and deny tourniquets of rescue

ode to soil

All that we do, all that we say or sing
Must come from contact with the soil.
– W.B. Yeats

ah   so often neglected
beggar woman
downtrodden
tattered
undernourished
dispirited

forgetting
a nurturer   mother
deserves rich gowns
plush velvet   garlanded
and jewelled
to be celebrated with lavish feasts
fallowed and rested

remembering
forests and flowers
revel in your kinship
singing for us at dawn
and again at dusk

ah   so often exploited
bleeding from wounds
we hear your cry on the wind
see your pain in our rivers

so often your cry of anguish silenced
your turmoil invisible

weary   neglected crone
is it yet too late
to feel our fingers
run through your hair
loving ourselves in you?

loud fence

ribbons fly from its wrought-iron facade
dangle from its posts
tied around its cast curves and arches
along its twisted columns
covering baroque-designed swirls

in silent protest
it shouts from its finials
that spear the sky

so many colours of so much pain
it screams in the wind
pierces like a metal bird's aborted launch
howls into hollowing darkness

in silent protest
wails in thunder and rain
stares out the still heat of day

louder & louder
with the mothers' sobbing
and children cowering

the fence yells
…and it yells

One way to find a voice when the cry for recognition and
forgiveness of systemic child abuse in churches and institutions goes
on deaf ears. Inspired by a Wilcox cartoon.

Hebrew Chorus

striding the beach with Spotify
my mind follows the story
imagines people huddled
trailing lines in exile
humming for courage
raw lament
for the destruction
of their temple   and the last smell
of their homeland   an old story
Verdi minds us not to repeat

back home   news flash
the Mariupol theatre   haunting
monochrome   old charm erased
two girls cower in a hint of iris blue
and sunflower in black rubble
charred husks
of ruined apartments
frame the screened nightmare
snow settles heavily
white-coated boughs trembling

i turn a smooth beach stone
over and over like a question
aching in my mind

gutted horror still plays
Nebuchadnezzar still lives

Chorus music from Verdi's opera Nambucco, the flight of people
after the destruction of the First Temple in Jerusalem in 586 BCE
In March 2022, a siege of Mariupol by Russian forces. Shelling
struck the ornate old theatre, reducing the building to rubble,
killing 600 people.

I can't breathe

mother earth is in pain
she shouts   cries   gasps
when will we listen?

to the shout in the fires
I can't breathe
with ash washed up on the beach
trees and koalas gone?

to the gasp in the pandemic
I can't breathe
the masks gagged
the vulnerable gone?

to the cry in the street
I can't breathe
equality ignored
of black lives matter

to the fish in our rivers
gasping for oxygen
farm chemicals
poison to our land

mother earth is in pain
she shouts   cries   gasps
when will we listen?

afterwards
15th October 2023

it is as if a forest gapes   exposed
sky often so blue growling grey
pungent air stifles breath

as if fire has devoured Country
ground of tiny orchids (gifts
of grace) gnashed in grief
questions sear like scars burnt
into memory
the tongues of eucalypts (that
i always understand) are tied in foetal
knots and a great silence falls over the land

the fall of tears like rain absolves
the blackened trunks of iron barks and
eucalypts cut the shadow side of beauty
slowly the howling wind softens
forest is heard with hymn of
yellow-green whispers
don't despair of being the witness
spirit is not spent
the tongues of eucalypts (that
i always understand) unfurl naked   sore
their sap murmurs today we begin again

Embracing life

song of birds
poetry flutters in me
urgent to be free

portal

a narrow passage
between two ironbarks

from hectic   loud air
into an earthy world

of closed-off skies
mossy sandstone caverns

moist soft tracks
each step cushioned

by sweet smelling
leaf mulch   so absorbing

i'm hardly here

this subtle cut
into another reality

like crossing over
to a liminal world

with life's great tumult
falling away

as bark falls from trees
seduces   slowly

to resolve
my restlessness

winter days

On the mudflats near an afternoon's silver lake, I stop to watch
a red dragon kite soar with dips and dives on whistling air.

>   a child again
>   neck crinked back
>   carefree

A fisherman and solitary figure on the dunes watch this
bird-like thing swirl and whirl. Purple ribbon tails flutter,
tangerine feathers swell, puffed up with air, tugging the string
the woman holds. I hum The Lark Ascending. I ask the
woman why she comes each afternoon.
She replies, because looking up makes me feel so much better.

>   one feather
>   holds the worrying day
>   lightly

decluttering

while hovering over a life of miscellany –
pruning a pile of diaries
lecture notes   travel journals
and sentimentality

letting go of keepsakes
into labelled boxes – staying…going…gone
i unearth a pile of letters and am startled by
my father's handwriting

my breathing changes rhythm
determined decluttering stops
i sit immersed in words of past springs
in this winter of life

so easy to like the yesterday   savour
its seasons   linger in its tangible
presence of acedia
cling to proof of its memory

but i shiver slightly having heard
a friend's life tumbled into a hired skip
a reminder doors close on cue
the wedge holding them an illusion of control

messages

a friend writes to me about observations
of how trees shed their bark   lemon
scenteds   scribblies   river reds   blue gums
how they let go of their old skin
some curling   some peeling in strips
some in patches like a jigsaw
i had never noticed this
caught only by colours of bark
and hint of new beginnings revealed

today we watch little wrens
dart along our track   flit onto branches
swing on blades of wild grass
some alight closer   tiny balls
of fluff   colours of almond and sky
their wink of tails
already pointy enough
to write their constant chirping
on the clouds

two willy wagtails hang
around   curators
of this escapade
and acrobatic swallows
are for now a spring song
of musical notes on a wire above
ever since the days when i read
the Native American Spirit Cards
i find messages in nature abound

like my grandma found reading tea leaves

wood pigeon

the glass door shuddered
a chill shot down my spine
a wood pigeon lay on the door step
i picked it up
cupped it in my two hands like this
alert to its rapid heart beat

ah the intimacy i felt
close to this normally aloof bird
I comforted its warm plump body
cooed to it like a bird whisperer
no way as serenely as it does to me
in the red-berried puriri tree at dusk

it stayed dazed for a short time
then slowly lifted its head as I stroked
down its iridescent green feathers
i like to think it felt safe

wings opened to full exquisite span
and from my hands it took flight

I thought as I watched it go free
what a privilege it was to hold
such beauty and strength
in my hands

sanctum

early in spring hearts are kindled
to protect a speck on our map –
an endangered breeding habitat

once a remote beach   Karagi Point
now marked by walkers and dogs –
environmentalists and council workers

mend fences   erect signs   and cctv
add driftwood shelters   sea grass
sand   small stones   shell   grit

thousands of kilometres away
hearts of little terns are also kindled
as instinct summons them to fly south

like sailors look to the night sky
little terns look to the warming air waves
with bodies light as a puff of cotton wool

their wiry wings brave buffet of wind
thrum of sea-ice   bitter cold –
lonely blue wipeout

frail and famished for fish
these sea warriors make landfall
to breed in our sanctum of welcome

epiphany

it happened as the day slowed
the still lake like a lullaby
soothing the eye's gaze

it erupted jet-like
into the grey-blue melding
of earth and sky amidst

reflected hills
that lazed in the lake
like a generous hug

trees   rocks   sand-islands
had forgotten themselves
in this misty blue daze

it happened with a harsh flutter
an epiphany
that split the quiet meniscus

as a huge cormorant surfaced
with an explosive spatter
struck up into the air

ragged black wings
long snake-neck   awkward shape
like an eruption from the underworld

its strange form aflutter
glistened in absolute black
lifted off

pierced the air
a plumed arrow   its shadow
crinkled on the once still lake

nankeen kestrel

out of a cloudless sky
it floats in a long rapture
its slender wings wide
exposing buff tawny lines

air its accompanist
in a Vaughan Williams waltz
tail aquiver like a prestissimo
conductor's baton

then it folds arrow-like
drops   a daunting drop
into the grassy dune
reappears
struggling prey gripped in a talon
balances on a fence post
takes off
a faint air brush on the sky

spellbound
in its aerial performance
we lose track of ourselves

it did not come for our pleasure
yet it was ours to behold
a brightness to marvel at
who can explain coincidence
even serendipity?

waiting for godwits

at a reedy edge of the lake –
a sanctuary for water birds
we are waiting for godwits to land
from their Arctic migration
a sylph-like bird with slender long legs
prying curved beak and noted
for its intrepid journey

we spend time observing littoral life
little terns shearwaters spoonbills egrets
watch five plover chicks tilt their heads
mimicking adult forage
note many duck species
ducklings tucked in their aura
grazing on the wrack

suddenly adult plovers with a wild screech
extend their wings
birds honk quack squawk
like whiffle balls wings fill the air

a dog
leaping wildly across the shallows
chases the fleeing birds
disturbing the sea grass
with its cache of crustaceans and insects
chases after any bird that dares to land
gallops like a crazed brumby back and forth
as its owner watches on

still mirrored lake   shattered
sanctuary ripped apart
churned like a miniature tsunami

finally the man whistles
gets on his bike and the big brown dog
sloshes out of the lake
my blazing eyes bore after them

i'm shattered like the lake   powerless
anger holding back tears

needing to be restored
i watch the birds settle back
on now stilled waters

delusions of grandeur

the ibis   tagged D44
rummages for crumbs
under our tables

then walks off
holding its head high
with a sense of self importance

as if it thinks
it is in a place where
they call it sacred

mirror on mirror

a blaze of red light
rebels along the horizon

soft pregnant hills
mirror deeply purple
in the silver shawl of lake
where pelicans graze
amongst the trees

as evening sun slips silently
behind sable cloud
the world holds its breath
like silence between two notes

we walk into the saffron
of winter light
with interplay of shade and shadow
while all around
birds fly home to their raucous
roosting in the palms

back in town a lone willy wagtail
struts backwards
and forward at a shop window
a spiegel im spiegel moment

joining the Arvo Pärt echoes
i too glance in the window
to the shock of my mother
reflected back
and the joy of one beside me
who could be his father

Murphy's law

they tumble from my bag
a tangle of earplug cables
chains cords keys frustration

with nimble fingers and eyes
of a forensic crime detective
i fumble to find their ends

an awkward tango one step
forward two steps back
enigma of beginnings and ends

ouroboros and Celtic coils
a new version of Murphy's law
anything that will tangle – will

even Christmas lights after a year
in the dark know Murphy
and his law emerging

as an amorphous jumble
to be unravelled   Murphy
knows no template

eve time

from the shaded terrace
i watch the maples and elms shy
like candles in an autumn breeze
the snuff of winter creeps through their veins

a call from my daughter –
excited by a day as relief teacher
at my old school –
she remembers it as a child
thought it bigger she laughs

i sit back in the chair drinking tea
ponder how friends and teachers
have passed on   no time to bridle
against change

i take great comfort from this view
on such a day as today
ready to meet winter

hold its sombre face
in the palms of my hands
and expect no smile
only twilight in its eyes

camouflage it by days of hot soup
and friends around the kitchen table
defy its lengthening shadow
with beanie and gloves for the garden
sometimes sprigs of spring in my mind
and in the eve time
music and books to soften it

its shivering chill I dismiss
ignore my goosebumps arms
time is short
shadows gather
there is much to do

bronze bells

of all the artefacts Marquis Yi of Zeng had buried with him –
bronze weapons   wine vessels   jewellery   jade and gold
marble statues   wooden tools even twenty sacrificed maidens

it is the room of bronze chime bells that rivets our attention
an orchestral set of sixty-five bells hanging from racks
patined by earth and age and still bearing a burnished

glint of fire that forged them in a bygone furnace
their ancient bronze   spiked   pocked   tuned in graven tones
to ring a king home to his heavenly splendour

today their knell is silent behind glass
no kiss awakens tinkling bells and groaning gongs
but here in Hubei Museum in a quiet insulated room

a time warp cracks
as five musicians with wooden mallets move around
a replica set of the bells   harmonise Frère Jacques
rebirthing the sound of antiquity

These 64 amazingly bells made in 433 BCE and were only unearthed in 1978. The tonal range of these ancient bells is from C2 to D7. In the middle area of the tonal range, it can play all twelve half tones. The wooden hammers used to strike the bells were also unearthed from the Zeng-hou-yi Tomb. The original bells are on permanent display at the Hubei Provincial Museum in Wuhan.

Two Canticles

At a cottage by the sea I tackle Francis Webb, curious about
his poetry from Cap and Bells. Outside a wild spring ocean's
curled waves tussle on the tide, comb to the edge, like spoonbills
probing every squint of sand and wrack. The horizon

is drawn-in, appropriate for this day in this ruptured world.
The sun finds thin spots to break through clouds, blades the sea
with thousands of stars and as quickly is blocked. In his poems
Francis tools words in obscurity and I must wait for the rare

glimmer to shine through, to touch their thousand stars before
they meld into his shadowed world. With torch and compass
I grope through the labours of Hospital Night and wait in the
dark for the sound of winged ones in the swaddled air of his

suite Ward Two. I once met a Benedictine nun who knew
Francis Webb, as an escapee from Parramatta Mental Hospital.
He knocked at her convent back door. Frail, lost, clutching
a book of poetry. Eyes eminently human, beaconed his ragged

struggle. His voice garbled: I am not seeking money or food
but peace. He scribbled out for her his poem Five Days Old.
Then a lonely, derelict figure slouched out the gate. His words
frisk the heroic-journey, explorers' struggle, like one who holds

a shell, turns it over and over for light, shots of colour, as he
tackles the one-journey common to us all. His poems of
The Canticle echo another Francis who wrote Il Cantico,
who praised glimpses of brother sun and sister moon through

tender, frayed clouds, who walked barefoot, high-walled Assisi:
its olive groves, vineyards, lanes, paths of cobbled stone,
searching too for peace. Falling on his knees, face in his hands
he humbly made himself its instrument, finding the meaning

only in the search. He threw off worldly garb, gold and plumes
donned a court jester's cap and bells, reverberating touch of
birdsong his bedrock. Through a darkling glass are two canticles
hundreds of years apart. Each Francis dances on fear's altar. Both

be fools, taunted, for gnawing life to the bone. Both seeing beauty
in the tiny not the immense. Outside, flocks of sea gulls skim
the southerly, skate on the edge. I listen to their skirl on the air,
wayfarers, like the ocean in its unceasing quest.

Embracing love

with family all around
my heart reaches out
to the one missing

a pelican-distance apart in covid times

i ramble the beach
where multi-hued shells dazzle
amongst the wink of quartz
along the littoral shore
pause to watch a small child
pile shells and stones
around a sandcastle
her young mum watching on

it's one of those August days
stretch of cobalt sky
not a trace of winter chill
we comment on how blessed we are

'i miss my mum' she says
having come from Dusseldorf
to marry and live in this paradise
i feel her helplessness –
in this once 'taken for granted' freedom
to travel the world

'i miss my daughter and
grandchildren in England' i say
shocked at the tear in my voice

masked we both stand
a pelican-distance apart
laugh at ourselves
struggling with our feelings
on this stunning day
at this stunning beach

'i wish I could hug you'
the young woman weeps
'i wish I could too'

we look out at the flush
of the distant horizon
mourning our loss
while the small carefree
unaware child plays on

A moment of serendipity. This was a time where travel was impossible and that connection we take so much for granted meant that there was a deep sense of separation felt between family members separated by travel.

conflagrations

this wild edge of the world explodes
into a great gulp of ocean
its headland barrier holds us lead-footed
in a full stop on our coastal walk

waves flare up
crash endlessly carving hard rock
thundering into empty coves below
while far out the ocean lulls

our little grandson lives on the periphery
pointing high   hypnotised
as shearwater gulls hover
wizards on the wing

his mind fired   alert to make-believe
dares the soaring birds   his shouts
lost in the ocean's acoustics
he is swashbuckling   a pirate

Ninja warrior of the ocean monsters
blue-ringed octopus his quest to conquer
whales for riding he says he sees
arms splayed in sweep of blond hair

we lose touch with his imaginings
fear the hard basalt edge –
where frustrations
can spark conflagration

flex our thoughts for action
as gleams of sun-splattered spindrift
shower the sky with tiny rainbows
and the tumble of waves

power back on themselves
where unpredictable conflagrations
go unquestioned

the visit

a daunting moment
a sudden confrontation
fight and flight at the same time

i close off 'in' doors
open wide the sliding door
wield a tea towel

it crashes the big sky window
hits the mirror and its reflection
the lost swallow grabs again

and again at the window
stunned   shocked
its beating against the glass

quickens my heart
then light as a black butterfly
it poises on the rim of a chair

close   we freeze
its throbbing bronze-red throat
sylphlike body stuns me –

the wonder of it
i feel it has sensed the wind
it opens pointed wings

stretches its tail   fork-like
a black-tipped arrow
homes out with acrobatic skill

dives   dips   darts   and i whisper
Hopkins' words   *ah! the achieve of,*
the mastery of the thing.

whisper

from my balcony i watch a friar bird
nestled high in the palm fronds
lay one egg a day for four days
each one is miracle enough
and in the dark of night
mother bird rests on her eggs
rising to sing in the dawn

the gardener comes
to clear spindly fronds
i shout down
over the chainsaw
'stop there is a nest here'
last evening i shooed away a crow
that landed on the palm eyeing the nest

how long to wait?
it says twenty-eight days gestation
then the chicks to rear!
how fragile is life
in a nest   in a manger
how fragile   how precious
is life in a refugee boat

fractured moonlight glints
from the dark of a broken world
my whisper of prayer
rising to sing in the dawn

tanka

a ladybug
lands on our picnic blanket
black dots on red
my grandson exclaims
I didn't know they were real

a meeting

How shall I walk in the world
But looking for light and wisdom
– Mary Oliver

you rise after rain
in autumnal mist
to walk out
and slow
not expecting to meet a prophet
calling in the wilderness
until you see
a hint of colour

Gulliver in Lilliput
you bend closer
your giant hands
part the grass
for secrets of the earth

stunned with humble beauty
the tiny mushrooms
slight and lowly
strong and perfect
caps intact
have pushed up
from the dung of darkness
smelling earthy and dank
their miniature purple parasols
with ivory ruffled collars
nod slightly quietly

on return the next day
there is only soggy earth
brambles and mulch of leaves
as if they had never been

while doing a grocery shop

you suggested buying flowers
i chose the day lilies
long slender stems tightly budded
their colour yet to be revealed

a navy blue vase
the last gift from my mother
i arranged them
to await the first peep of colour

they would open as they chose
we patiently watered   waited
worked and dined
at the table with them

the buds stirred
blossomed   each a surprise
some yellow   some white
lightly red-speckled petals

every time i noticed them
they made me smile
you suggested buying flowers –
that has doubled the pleasure

shared umbrella

so much is gained
by

a shared umbrella
with

synchronicity
of gait

besides the intimacy
of leaning in

diagnosis

away from its rooms
        down the lift to the car park
        pay the ticket to release the boom gate
into the coffee shop   its clutter of cups and chatter
and coffee aroma to fill my air deafen my mind

away from the fitted slots of diagnoses
        black texta pens   x marks the spot
        and wield of needle   scan   knife and life
escaping the monster that unleashes poison
the despot of cancer that preys for victims

running from its panting
        its imprisoning tentacles
        its googled-fear
and into a sky that is bluer today
i remember my friend said

when she was unshackled
        she felt humble
        grateful
Now her words release the tears
that wash away walls and floors

wood glue and cement
        room by room
        in a slow and steady flow
and like the magpies in a nearby branch
I find I can warble again

presence

when i turn back for the last time the old
armchair looks up like a wise storyteller   its
arms settled and wide   its high back pressed

against the wall and softly cushioned
its William Morris bird fabric tattered
in places   threadbare in others   faded

red cherries in its design still smile
of summer   i hear the static hiss of the
gramophone and remember the shy

swan lost in its reflection till it escapes
in the Tchaikovsky dance   the light
shadows in from an ivy framed door

a scatter of sparrows   brown darting
puffballs in the grass   still wait on the
ritual of Nanna shaking out crumbs

from the tablecloth   around me
in the room there hangs a presence
as if the stories of the Pied Piper and

Lady of Shallot burst like fruit ripe for tasting
and no one there to taste   if only i could tell
the chair the adventures and discoveries

it has given are packed tight in my knapsack
and feels light as music   if i could tell it
of the life it has gifted me –

without it i wouldn't be setting out
knowing as i open the door the air will
howl in like it does into an empty space

petal by petal

for Pat

1

i take flowers that day
tight buds of pink roses
to light up the room

trim and arrange them
a few sprigs of greenery from her courtyard
forgetting she can't see

this woman   who said she had eyes
in the back of her head
stares vacantly at faces

in PPE   masks   helmet shields
familiar voices
her only connect

the room   alien territory
could be a space ship
for her the air so thin

she listens to the rosary on her audio
attempts to mouth the Gloria song
at the end of each set

days fall away
waiting like blooms
for nature's whisper

2

amidst roses and thorns
and clutter of life's things
books   umbrellas   tea cups

that life's ripening brings
essentials once
now barely

a sponge   lip balm
holding of a hand   touch
delicate as tracery of a veined leaf
the unknown
softened for us
by whorl and curl of petals –

our eyes drawn
as to a lighthouse
on a treacherous night

3

she says in a wearied voice
eyes closed
there are smiling faces

on the wall
i ask if she knows them
she doesn't answer

the hedge outside
with mock-orange fragrance
leans in   watchful

only sometimes
and that sometimes
is rarely

there is a land
where we travel
to times edge

edge of all there is
so brutal and alive –
it is its own being

4

how slowly blossoms fall
petal by petal
fall scattered on the dresser

even in stillness
labour of breath silent
the room is full of her

we sit like creatures
stranded on rock
the touch of her hand in mine

gone…i let go
watch dawn-light transfigure
an empty vase

his favourite shirt

i.m. Fr. Otto Shelley SVD

how often i followed it on bush treks
its blue-green check flannel
faded   threadbare
just ahead
striding out
with slight stoop
pointing the way

ready to classify
this tree   that plant
finding   connections
in nature's woven web

check the leaf pattern
note the nodes
the venation

and bent over
his favourite shirt
a familiar friend
he searched for seed pods and
patterns   clues of life

stretching up
pondering
always pressing onward

the moment
i turn to follow
he is gone

maybe a cypher

when the vet made a home visit
to euthanise my dog
then carried her lifeless body away
backyard birds stopped singing

air muffled like sitting in a padded
sound-proof box
life stilled
even restless leaves hushed

i made a coffee
and sat at the kitchen table
three pigeons waggled over
up the steps at the back door

their wings fanning out
feathers iridescent in a sun-ray
their cooing a song of lament
not heard before

they came so close
onto the top step
maybe they thought me a statue
did they feel the energy?

did they know their gentle old friend
had left ? did they know I was bereft?
they lingered as if waiting
upon sadness

reminder

air is riven with grief   a low
slow pall of whispers   shrouds
our small communal world

heads shake in disbelief
gasping sounds like that of fish
stranded at low tide

yet in this laden torpor
cicadas still ring their song
timid blue-hearted pansies nod

and in a corner of her garden
a young hibiscus bursts
into flower   its yellow suns

quivering with search for meaning
as today at the funeral
many search for words of comfort

dragonflies on the mirrored
surface of our loss   and from
a screen   memories draw us in

her toasting with wine laughter play
arms lovingly encircled
hugs of celebrations

to a backdrop of a tended garden
multi-coloured petunias
rambling golden roses
that give and give

this is life it is beautiful
it reminds us of the fable
where a fish asks 'where is the sea?'

and the wise fish answers 'you're in it!'
back at home the sweet scent
of camellias wafts from her garden

songlines

trace the spirit of land
follow rivers
landscapes
soils
cool springs
star maps

listen to song
navigate seasonal
changes   early farming
care of country
reconnect ourselves

the earth is our mother –
mother of all
says Hildegard of Bingen
from the twelfth century
across the cultures
she cradles   succours us

settle to the space between
your breaths   listen to the silence
between heart beats   hear the
whisper of earth   tread lightly
we walk sacred ground

From the Dust of Stars

A keke-ke-ik cry skirls the air, not from the lone
gull high in the green cloud, not the cormorant fishing
the lake in early light, nor from swallows in their
scythe and skim at the edge but a pair of plovers
on the bank, their urgent call in rhythm with
the pace of circus stilt-walkers on red legs.

Spurred wings swoop low in pursuit–
qui vive their defence of nest and chicks hidden in
verge of bristled grass. Strategically, they strut
grim-masked faces, sometimes coy in priested–collar
sometimes they stretch their white necks and shriek
like angry roosters. I sense their desperation

and step back to honour their cry.
Plover instinct jolts my mind to parenthood.
Memory of a little one, nuzzled at the breast, hand
curved, warm skin to skin swaddled in the pre-dawn.
Now my eyes stay on these ground birds.
I muse how we come from the dust of stars fired

from the same exploding cosmos.
A clear morning opens into the sky. A new day –
joggers, walkers some with dogs on leads,
picnickers, fishermen, all possible intruders
keep the plovers on the alert. A black crow waits
on a nearby branch, its eye a laser beam.

Celtic Knots

The table and oil crayons gleam in the early sun.
My granddaughter's eyes shine a warm welcome.

She is waiting to teach me to draw a Celtic Knot.
It is June and English spring gardens, left for rewilding

are blazing with flowers and weeds, bees and butterflies:
the result of 'No Mow May' and are so delightful, no-one

seems to have the heart to return to manicured lawns.
Blue Tits are coming and going to a nesting box.

Yesterday my daughter beckoned me to come close
and listen to the baby-twitching-world inside.

Today I follow my granddaughter's instructions, beginning
with a pentagon and follow her lines as winding as walking

a labyrinth, until voilà ! It all connects. Our shading makes
it deeply three dimensional. She is eight, I am almost eighty.

Our paths have crossed only four times since I helped
my daughter bring her into the world. But our bond

twines like a Celtic Knot even though our connecting
is mostly two screens quavering over FaceTime.

I won't be here when the lessons coil like snakes
and she learns that beginnings become endings.

I won't be here to remind her that endings are beginnings.
I think about what is to become of our world and I can't grasp

her innocence in it. I watch her small hand drawing confidently.
Love is the absence of fear, mystic Julian of Norwich reminds us.

Again my daughter calls us outside to the garden to watch
two fledgling balls of feathers fluttering in the apple tree.

We three stand, entwined arm in arm. Endings
seem far away.

Acknowledgments

'Two Canticles' first place in the Philippa Holland Poetry Award, Eastwood/Hills FAW Writers National Poetry Competition. 2024. Published in the Rochford Street Review, Issue 40, 2024:2 ed. Linda Adair and Mark Roberts.

'Fifth symphony', Highly Commended in Poetica Christi *Press Poetry Competition 2024*

published in A New Day Dawns, Poetica Christi Press 2024 ed. Janette Fernando

'From the Dust of Stars', Short listed in SWW National Writing Competition 2023. Published in Spiritus: *A Journal of Christian Spirituality*, John Hopkins University Press Vol 24, No 1, Spring 2024. To be reprinted in *Ink 4 SWW Centenary Anthology 2025* .

'Petal by Petal', Short listed in SWW National Writing Competition 2022. To be reprinted in Ink *4 SWW Centenary Anthology 2025.*

'Afterwards' in *Telling Australia's Truth.* Poems selected by Stephen Matthews, Ginninderra Press 2024

'Le Ciel' featured in double fold of my poetry in Womens Ink Winter issue 2024 in a feature Art and Artists ed Jan Conway

'Loud Fence' in Mozzie Vol. 31 Issue 4 December 2023.ed. Ron Heard

Haiku in *Under the Same Moon.* Fourth Haiku Anthology ed. by Lyn Reeves, Vanessa Proctor and Rob Scott March 2024 and in Echidna Tracks 2024. ed. Lynette Arden

Tanka published in Eucalypt ed Julie Thorndyke 2024

'winter days' published as a haibun in The Blue Heron Spring 2023

'Daybreak at Mt. Sondar (Rwetyepme)' and 'wood pigeon' are earlier award winning poems.

I am grateful to the editors for their encouragement and dedication to poetry.

Thank you to Norm Neill and poets of the Tuesday Poetry Group at NSW Writers Centre, Roselle and to David Atkinson and Pennant Hills Poets (PHP) for their positive critique, affirmation and keeping me on task.

Warm appreciation to Pip Griffin for her final edit of my work and for her friendship. I especially appreciate her generosity, her time and her editing skills.

My loving appreciation to Michael for his constant presence and inspiration.

www.ingramcontent.com/pod-product-compliance
Lightning Source LLC
Chambersburg PA
CBHW071904070526
44583CB00016B/1839